Cayman Islands

Simple Travel Guide

Table of Contents

General Information

The Cayman Islands belong to the British Overseas Territories and are located on three islands in the western Caribbean. The largest island, Grand Cayman, is famous for its sea resorts and places for diving. On the island of Cayman Brac, tourists are offered to go deep-sea fishing. On the small island of Little Cayman, iguanas live, as well as seabirds.

Perhaps the most amazing thing in all the Caribbean islands is their dissimilarity to each other, despite the small distance between them. So, the Cayman Islands are a special place with their reefs, beaches with colorful sand and mangroves along the edge of the coast.

- *Capital - Georgetown*
- *Language - English*
- *Currency - Cayman Islands Dollar*
- *Time Zone - GMT -5*
- *Population - 54,000*
- *Territory - 264 km²*
- *Emergency (telephone) – 911*

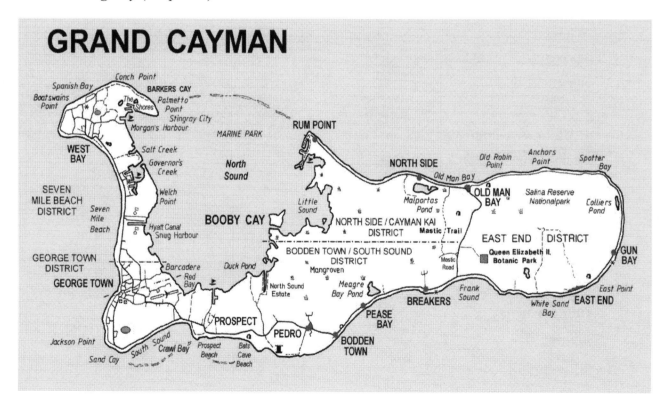

10 facts about the Cayman Islands

1. The Cayman Islands are one of the fourteen sovereign territories of Great Britain but are not part of the United Kingdom.
2. The Cayman Islands are known not only as a prosperous offshore zone but also as one of the prestigious resorts. First, the islands are famous for their beautiful beaches, which create ideal conditions for spearfishing and diving.
3. The Cayman Islands have one of the highest per capita income indicators. And this is so even though most of the goods on the islands have to be imported.
4. The highest point of the islands is 42 meters. It is located on the island of Cayman Brac, along which a limestone plateau stretches.
5. There are no rivers in the Cayman Islands, while the interior of the islands has swampy areas.
6. The terrestrial vegetation and wildlife of the Cayman Islands is not diverse, which cannot be said for the reefs surrounding the islands. Here, fish, turtles, mollusks, and crustaceans are found in a wide variety.
7. When Christopher Columbus discovered two of the three Cayman Islands in 1503, they were called Las Tortugas, which meant "turtles". The discoverers gave this name to the islands because they saw a huge number of turtles on them. In 1523, the Cayman Islands began to be called Lagartos ("big lizards", or "alligators"). This name was because the Europeans who saw large lizards on the islands and mistook them for crocodiles.
8. The islands were inhabited only at the end of the XVIII - beginning of the XIX century. Prior to this, the territory served as a transit point for sailors, as well as pirates. Because of this, a population of turtles was almost destroyed on the islands, but now there is the only tortoise farm in the world that annually releases thousands of turtles into the sea!
9. There are legends that many famous pirates visited here and were even buried here with their myriad treasures. Surely, for this reason, many curious tourists are trying to look for pirate treasures.
10. The Cayman Islands experience the power of the most powerful Atlantic hurricanes. According to statistics, powerful hurricanes hit the islands every two and a half years.

How much does a vacation in the Cayman Islands cost?

The cost of rest in the Cayman Islands is the sum of the cost of air travel, food, and accommodation. I must say that the prices here are very high, so a tour of the Cayman Islands will be an expensive undertaking.

Air flight. To get to the Cayman Islands you have to fly with a transfer through Europe, Canada or the USA. A two-way ticket will cost at least USD 1,000 (if you fly from Europe). For US residents, this amount is much lower.

Hotels. Living in the Cayman Islands is expensive. A room even in the simplest hotel will be around USD 100 per night.

Food. The average check at restaurants in the Cayman Islands will be from USD15-20. However, there is just an opportunity to save money and join the local cuisine at the same time, if you change restaurants to cafes and small street food stalls near markets. By the way, the choice of products in the markets is also quite good.

Thus, you will have to pay USD 2,000-3,000 for 1 week / 2 persons

Hotels in the Cayman Islands

The best hotels in the Cayman Islands are located in the main city, Georgetown. It is here that luxurious five-star hotels are located that offer luxury vacations.

I advise you to pay attention to The Ritz-Carlton, Grand Cayman (apartments for USD 380 per night). The hotel is located right on the beach, allowing you to fully appreciate all the magic of the Caribbean. The journey to the local airport will take you only 10 minutes!

Among the accommodation options of this class, there are several more interesting places. This is Le Soleil d'Or, which is located in the resort of The Mornings. Booking a room will cost about USD 500. But you can relax on the private beach or near the outdoor pool, or go to the spa.

For those who are not so principled in choosing the category of the hotel to stay, there are wonderful four-star offers. Grand Cayman Marriott Beach Resort collected many positive reviews. A double room can be rented for USD 170.

A hotel of the same level at Sand Bluff, Wyndham Reef Resort, Grand Cayman, will offer accommodation for USD 126. For your convenience, most apartments have a kitchenette, so this offer is ideal for families.

One has only to look at the photos of the Grand Cayman Beach Suites, and you will understand that this is a paradise on earth. You will live in a luxury complex on Seven Mile Beach and enjoy the wonderful scenery every morning!

Finding low-priced deals in the Cayman Islands will not be easy. But the sooner you start your search, the more chances you will have! For example, booking apartments at Will T Place will cost $ 80. To do this, you will need to go to Lower Valley.

But if you intend to live in the capital, then it is better to choose a 2-star hotel Comfort Suites Seven Mile Beach and Resort for USD 102. For approximately the same price, you can stay at the Holiday Inn Resort Grand Cayman.

Public transport and car rental

Public transport in the Cayman Islands includes taxis and domestic airlines. You can get between the islands, the distance between which is more than one hundred kilometers, only by local airlines. Cayman Airways, Cayman Airways Express, and Island Air are active in the Cayman Islands.

Taxis in the Cayman Islands are the most convenient way to get around. The car can be ordered by phone, caught on the street or near the hotel. Some hotels have their taxi fleet. A taxi ride in the Cayman Islands will cost $ 10, baggage allowance - $ 1.25, waiting - $ 0.65 per minute.

There is a car rental point in the Cayman Islands in Georgetown. It is worth considering that car rental in the Cayman Islands allows you to move by car only on the island of Grand Cayman. The other two islands can be reached either by plane or by sea.

To rent a car in the Cayman Islands, you must be over 21 years old, have an international driver's license, as well as a local driving license issued in a rental office (to purchase it you will need to show a driver's license and pay about USD 8). Car rental prices in the Cayman Islands, as elsewhere in the Caribbean, are quite high. You have to pay from USD 100for a day.

Rules of the road in the Cayman Islands:

- Left-hand traffic
- Safety belts must be fastened
- Overtaking is permitted only on the left side.
- The dipped-beam headlights must be switched on in the evening and at night, as well as in conditions of poor visibility on the roads
- The permissible level of alcohol in the driver's blood is 0.5 ppm

Speed limit in the Cayman Islands:

- in the village - 40-50 km / h
- outside the village - 60-80 km / h

Customs Rules

The Cayman Island Customs is governed by the traditional rules of the Caribbean, adjusted for its characteristics.

1. What can I bring to the country by plane:

- Any amount of national and foreign currency
- For persons over the age of 18 years, up to 200 cigarettes or 50 cigars, or 0.5 pounds (250 grams) of tobacco
- Meat products in factory packaging costing no more than USD 35
- Personal items

2. What is prohibited to import into the Cayman Islands:

- Living plants
- Beef
- Raw fruits and vegetables
- Perishable Products
- Drugs and drug-containing medications
- Fake coins
- Gambling tools and devices
- Weapons, ammunition, and explosives (gunpowder) are imported only with the permission of the special authorized police
- Pets without permission from the Department of Agriculture of the Islands.

3. What is forbidden to export from the Cayman Islands:

- Lobster
- Shells and mollusk meat (an exception is made for transit passengers)
- Protected representatives of marine and terrestrial flora and fauna (including tropical birds)
- Antiquities (including those found at the bottom of the sea) and antiques (special permission is required confirming the legality of their purchase and export from the country)

4. How much alcohol I can bring to the Cayman Islands:

- Up to 1 quart (0.95 liters) of alcoholic drinks (including wine)
- Up to three liters of any drinks

5. How much alcohol can be exported from the country:

- Up to three liters of any drinks

Currency exchange

Cayman Islands Dollar (KYD; CI $), equal to 100 cents. In circulation are banknotes in denominations of 100, 50, 25, 10, 5 and 1 dollar, as well as coins in denominations of 25, 10, 5 and 1 cent.

The Cayman Islands dollar is pegged to the US dollar at a fixed rate (CI $ 1 = $ 1.25), although the banking rate usually differs slightly from the officially set one. US dollars are freely traded on the islands and are accepted for payment or exchanged at most banks and commercial establishments.

Banks and currency exchange

Banks are open Monday through Thursday, from 9.00 to 16.00, on Fridays - from 09.00 to 16.30. Some banks are open on Saturdays from 9.00 to 12.00-13.00.

Currency can be exchanged at banks, hotels and specialized exchange offices located at the airport and in many banks of the capital. Banks usually offer a slightly better rate for all types of currencies (it is simply impossible to exchange any of the European or Asian currencies outside their borders, while US dollars are accepted everywhere without conversion).

Most hotels, travel agencies and rental companies accept credit cards from leading global payment systems. ATMs located in most banking offices throughout the country, as well as in ports and airports, work with Visa, MasterCard and Cirrus cards. However, in some small restaurants, hotels, and cafes, especially in Little Cayman and Cayman Brac, it is extremely difficult to use credit cards.

Carnivals and festivals

Grand Cayman celebrates two main holidays, the Batabano Carnival (April) and the Pirate Week (late October - mid-November). The Batabano festival takes place on Easter weekend throughout the island. This is a real national event, accompanied by many costumed processions and theatrical performances - a huge number of tourists visit the islands during the festival to see one of the most colorful holidays in the region. Its equivalent on the island of Cayman Brac is known as Braccanal and is held a week later.

Pirate Week is a historic theatrical carnival, which is accompanied by fireworks, parades, street dance events, theatrical sea battles and other attributes of "pirate life." Following the roar and thunder of the "pirate invasion" and the parade of ships held on the first Saturday of the festival, the whole country organizes various cultural heritage festivals for almost 11 consecutive days (held in almost every rural area), Caribbean music evenings, cultural heritage days of various regions, elections "Miss Festival", festivals of pirate and folk music, various sports events.

Every week in June, a weekly fishermen's tournament is held, where locals and visitors to the islands test their skills in fishing and a variety of seafood. Prizes for record copies caught at these competitions are also rather big in cash! Immediately after him, a two-day competition for the prize of the Cayman Culinary Society (CCS) usually begins, followed by the election of the cook of the year, bartenders and a large trade fair.

Useful Travel Tips

The following points should be considered when traveling to the Cayman Islands:

1. The inhabitants of the Cayman Islands are conservative, and public displays of passion are not welcome here.

2. Camping is prohibited on the territory of the Cayman Islands. The consequence of a tent on the shore may be imprisonment.

3. Underwater hunting and taking to the surface any form of marine life, including empty shells and dead coral branches, is prohibited in the Cayman Islands.

4. All tap water in the country is obtained by the distillation of the sea and is safe to use. However, I recommend drinking bottled water.

5. Payphones are ubiquitous and work on prepaid cards sold at company offices, post offices, newsstands, and shops.

6. Most hotels, shops and travel agencies accept credit cards from leading global payment systems. ATMs are ubiquitous.

7. In Little Cayman and Cayman Brac, it is better to pay in cash, a terminal may be absent here.

8. Travel checks can be cashed at most major stores, hotels, as well as at banks and travel agencies. Checks are best taken in US dollars.

9. On the islands, there are many Duty-Free shops where you can purchase goods without customs duties.

10. Jamaican dollars can be imported to the territory of the Cayman Islands in an amount of no more than JAD 20.

10 MUST DO!

1. Wander through the winding streets of Georgetown.

2. Buy gifts at the casemates of the former Old Court Building in Georgetown.

3. Drive along the underwater part of the Cayman Islands on the Atlantis tourist submarine.

4. Visit the castle of Pedro St. James in the Savannah.

5. Search for treasures in the Pirate Caves.

6. Conquer the waves of the Caribbean on a surfboard.

7. Scuba dive to the beauties of local coral reefs.

8. Admire the green turtles at the Cayman Islands Turtle Farm.

9. Feed the stingrays on the North Wall and Stingray Sandbar reefs.

10. Try the tortoise soup!

When is the best time to travel to the Cayman Islands?

The high season in the Cayman Islands falls from November to April. The weather at this time is not too hot, the maximum temperature during this period is +24 C. This is exactly the time when it is best to relax in the Cayman Islands. The weather is dry, there is almost no rain, and you can swim.

But during the low season in the Cayman Islands, from May to October, tropical showers rage. Although they are usually short-lived, high humidity combined with heat is not the time to go to the Cayman Islands.

Winter

The temperature ranges from +17 to +24 C almost all winter in the Cayman Islands. The bathing season does not stop at this time. The weather in the Cayman Islands is dry in winter, which allows you to fully explore the islands and try all kinds of local entertainment.

December

Holidays in the Cayman Islands in December fall on the most favorable time of the year for recreation and the peak of the tourist season. The weather at this time is warm, the air temperature reaches +24 C, allowing you to swim, surf and dive, and explore local attractions. Tours to the Cayman Islands in December for Christmas holidays are especially popular. After all, the Cayman Islands have taken a lot from English traditions, and they love Christmas very much and celebrate it on a grand scale.

January

January is the coldest month of the year, around +20 C. The sea is usually warmer, and travelers continue to swim, especially on the coast of Ram Point, in the southern part of Grand Cayman.

However, the cool weather does not make holidays in the Cayman Islands in winter worse. Reef diving, surfing and the amazing places of the Cayman Islands, which you can go sightseeing, make it truly fascinating. You can take a plane to Little Cayman to its bird sanctuaries, or visit a turtle farm, or arrange an adventure in the Pirate Caves - all this is possible during a tour to the Cayman Islands in January. And in January they celebrate New Year and National Heroes Day.

February

Holidays in the Cayman Islands in February will allow you to move into the summer in the middle of winter. The air temperature reaches +24 C, you can swim or sunbathe on the beaches covered with white and black sand, you can go scuba diving to explore, or you can take a walk through the museums and historical monuments of the Cayman Islands.

For example, look at the National Gallery of the Cayman Islands and get acquainted with the work of local artists. Tours to the Cayman Islands in February are popular with tourists from around the world. February here is the middle of the high season, and therefore there will be many vacationers at this time.

Spring

Most of the spring the Cayman Islands is great for relaxing. Weather in the Cayman Islands in the spring is warm, the air temperature practically does not differ from the winter, there is no rain. But the second half of April is the time when the heat begins. In May, it reaches +30 C, and at the same time showers begin. So, it's better to plan a trip to the Cayman Islands in the first half of spring.

March

Holidays in the Cayman Islands in March are almost the best time option that you can think of on the archipelago. At this time, the temperature rarely drops below +24 C, so you can not only surf or sail but also swim in the warm Caribbean Sea. In addition, vacation in the Cayman Islands in the spring is a great opportunity to visit the islands of Little Cayman and Cayman Brac with their natural parks and noisy bird flocks.

April

Holidays in the Cayman Islands in April fall immediately on two of the island's much-loved holidays. We are talking about the Batabano Carnival, during which the country for several days turns into a real extravaganza of colors, music, and dance. This is one of the most important festivals of the archipelago, so if you were lucky enough to get to it during your holidays in the Cayman Islands in the spring, you can fully find out how the local people have fun. And the second Monday of April is an unofficial holiday in the Cayman Islands in honor of the Queen's birthday.

Beach tours to the Cayman Islands in April are very popular because many tourists seek to have time to plunge into the Caribbean before the rainy season.

May

Holidays in the Cayman Islands in May fall at the beginning of the tropical rainy season. The air temperature at this time reaches +30 C. It rains every day, and even a short rain has time to wet everything around.

The soil in the Cayman Islands is swampy, so everything here is soaring rapidly. And walking deep into the islands while relaxing in the Cayman Islands in late spring quickly becomes difficult. And the combination of heat with high humidity does not contribute to the popularity of tours to the Cayman Islands in May.

Summer

In summer, the tropical rainy season begins on the archipelago. Showers rain on cities and beaches every day. The weather in the Cayman Islands in summer is hot (+30 C). In combination with humidity, this gives a very difficult climate, unsuitable for recreation.

June

Holidays in the Cayman Islands in June fall during the period of tropical showers. Even the short duration of showers does not make holidays in the Cayman Islands in summer especially comfortable. Humidity combined with the heat of +30 C makes rest at this time very difficult. Among other things, during a tour to the Cayman Islands in June, you have a chance to meet a storm or a hurricane. These weather events often make the weather non-flying, and flights to Little Cayman and Cayman Brac are often canceled and delayed.

July

During a vacation in the Cayman Islands in July, you have a chance to see a tropical rainfall. This is a grandiose sight - the wall of water flowing from the sky looks impressive. However, the riot of nature can greatly spoil your vacation in the Cayman Islands in the summer.

Although it does not rain for long, the air temperature of +30 C is difficult to tolerate in high humidity. But the warm water of the Caribbean is guaranteed. So, a beach tour in the Cayman Islands in July can be done pretty well, especially if you follow the weather forecast.

August

If you want to see all the riot of the summer tropical elements with showers, storms, and hurricanes, then a vacation in the Cayman Islands in August will undoubtedly suit you. Especially if you carefully monitor the weather forecasts in order to have time to swim before it starts to rain.

True, walks in nature parks while relaxing in the Cayman Islands in the summer will be quite difficult. The swampy land of the archipelago is very wet with rains, and you are unlikely to get pleasure from such a trip. Tours to the Cayman Islands in August are more suitable for extreme people, however, many tourists still come here at this time.

Autumn

it rains in the Cayman Islands almost half the fall. But already in the second half of October, the heat gradually begins to subside, and the sky lightens. Weather in the Cayman Islands in the fall tends to a little bit of winter, and the temperature reaches + 17-24 C. Since then, rest in the Cayman Islands becomes quite comfortable.

September

Rest conditions in the Cayman Islands in September are no different from the summertime. The heat is still there, reaching +30 C, tropical rain falls regularly, and sometimes hurricanes and storms occur. The sea often storms, so many yachting trips are curtailed, just as dives on the Atlantis submarine. However, the water at this time is very warm, so it's quite possible to arrange a beach tour to the Cayman Islands in September if you carefully monitor the weather.

October

During a vacation in the Cayman Islands in October, the period of tropical showers gradually ends. The heat subsides, the sea calms down, hurricane winds are replaced by a breeze. And in the second half of October, swimming, riding the waves and traveling around the Cayman Islands becomes quite comfortable.

The best time to take a tour to the Cayman Islands in October starts from the second week of the month. At this time, the Pirate Week starts here, the brightest festival of the year, when there is a lot of fun with music, dancing and fireworks! Skipping this festival is simply unthinkable!

November

This is the beginning of the high season. It is warm here at this time, the air temperature reaches +24 C. Swimming in the turquoise waters of the Caribbean Sea, the opportunity of scuba diving to explore coral reefs and sunken ships and exploring local sights make a vacation in the Cayman Islands truly magical in the fall!

The Cayman Islands Regions

The regions of the Cayman Islands are divided directly by the islands of the archipelago. The islands are divided into seven districts, five of which are located on the island of Grand Cayman, one on the island of Cayman Brac and one on the island of Little Cayman. The names of the regions of the Cayman Islands most often refer to the cardinal points or have a historical origin. There are few cities in the regions of the Cayman Islands - the capital, Georgetown, the former capital of Bodden, Savannah, East End, and Northside.

Grand Cayman Regions

Bodden Town. The center of the region is the old capital of the Cayman Islands, the city of Bodden. Here, as elsewhere on the archipelago, there are beaches suitable for swimming and surfing, as well as the famous Pirate Caves, now turned into an attraction for tourists.

East End. The region occupies the eastern part of the island. Here is the resort town of East End, around which there are many convenient beaches. And here you can get acquainted with the traditional life of the islanders.

Georgetown. The region is formed around the eponymous capital of the archipelago. There are many attractions, in particular, the fort of the islands, preserved from the XVIII century. Also in the city is the main port of the Cayman Islands.

Northside. The region occupies the northeastern part of the island. The beaches here mostly have black sand, which is especially picturesque. The center of the region is the city with the same name, one of the resort centers of the archipelago.

West Bay. The region occupies the western part of the island. The beaches here are with white sand, and the whole atmosphere of the classic coral coast is fully preserved.

Little Cayman Region

Little Cayman Island is located in a separate region. The small island is 130 km from Grand Cayman. Locals work exclusively in tourism. Here you will find pristine nature with classic mangroves and many animal species. You will especially enjoy many birds on the island. The island is home to the Birdy Pound Nature Reserve National Bird Sanctuary.

Cayman Brac Regions

The region completely occupies the entire island of Cayman Brac - the smallest and wildest of the islands of the archipelago, densely overgrown with fruit trees, orchids, and cacti and surrounded by excellent beaches. Here are the Cayman Brac Museum, the gardens of Christopher Columbus Park, Peter Cave Caves (in the northeast), Great Cave (at the southeastern tip of the island), Bat Cave, Scall Cave, and Rebecca Cave, as well as Park Community and Parrots National Park.

Grand Cayman

Grand Cayman Island (Grand Cayman) is the largest, most populated and most developed island of the archipelago. For a long time, it was famous for only two of its sights - 300 offshore banks and excellent conditions for scuba diving. However, it has now become one of the most popular resort areas in the region.

This small island has a diverse natural environment. Its rounded eastern part has slightly indented coasts framed by a thick wall of ancient coral reefs. The western part has a very indented coastline, where the sea extends inland with many winding bays, lagoons adapted for yacht parking and ports. The coral barrier is practically absent here, and the great depths of the sea allow even large ocean vessels to approach the shore. It is here that the best beaches on the island, the international airport, as well as many resorts are located.

Georgetown

The capital of the Cayman Islands, the administrative center of the territory and its main port - Georgetown (George Town), located on the west coast of Grand Cayman. A fairly small, but colorful and modern city is built as if especially in sharp contrast. The old part of the city is low houses similar to colonial mansions or tropical bungalows. It is enough to walk along Miles Road and go to Miles Crescent to see the most characteristic features of local urban planning.

The new part of the city looks completely different. Ultramodern houses, duty-free shops. Every week, cruise ships land thousands of passengers in Georgetown Harbor!

The sights of Georgetown are standard for the capitals of the island states of the Caribbean Sea and include a modest historical center, which has been kept practically unchanged since the end of the XVIII century. Fragments of Fort George Fortress (1790) rise above the harbor.

National Museum of the Cayman Islands (open on weekdays from 9:00 to 17:00, on Saturdays - from 10:00 to 14:00, entrance - CI $ 4) is located in the oldest building of the city - Old Court Building. This 150-year-old building served as a court, a prison, a dance hall, and even a temple, and in 1990 it was restored and turned into a museum (a gift shop is located in the prison's casemates), considered one of the best in the region. The collection of the National Museum contains more than four thousand exhibits from different historical eras, starting with various attributes of colonial rule and an extensive collection of coins raised from wrecks, and ending with an extensive collection of historical documents and maps.

A few blocks north of the museum stands the Elmslie Memorial Church, built in 1920 by the architect and shipbuilder Ryan (ship motifs are clearly visible in the appearance of the building).

To the south of the museum, you can find the colorful small Panton Square, immediately beyond which the city suburbs begin.

And to the north stretches the Harbor Drive promenade, on which the city church and Church Hall are located.

A little northeast, if you go along Fort Street, is the modern building of the Legislative Assembly, reminiscent of a truncated pyramid (the very first building made of monolithic concrete on the island). Next door is another Ryan building, Peace Memorial Town Hall, which is used today as one of the premises of the city court. Across the street, on Edward Street, there is another work of the same architect - the Church-like Public Library, which contains a large collection of books about the Cayman Islands, with a small bookstore. Nearby are the city chimes, and a little lower on the same street is the building of the General Post Office (1939) and a little to the east - Elizabeth Square. Edward Street goes into the winding Elgin Avenue, where you can see the police headquarters, a complex of government agencies, the buildings of the immigration and tourism departments, as well as the picturesque Cricket Square. And Cardinal Avenue stretches west of the Main Post Office with its countless duty-free shops.

The Cayman Maritime Museum of Treasures on North Church has an extensive diorama dedicated to the days when the islands were one of the centers of navigation, as well as a unique "automated guide" - the Blackbird cybernetic system, which tells stories "about the past of the Cayman Islands.

Also noteworthy is the National Gallery of the Cayman Islands with an extensive collection of works by local and foreign authors.

Cardinal Park on Courts Road is a private collection of animals and plants that can be found on the islands.

South Church Street has a small beach near Eden Rock where you can rent snorkeling equipment and dive into one of the island's most beautiful reefs.

The Atlantis tourist submarine is based in the same area for 48 people (Atlantis Adventures office is located on South Church Street, the cost of diving is about $ 70-85 per person for a group tour and $ 395 for two when diving to great depths).

Around the Georgetown

On the northeast side of the island, you will find the resort towns of Savannah, Bodden, East End, and Northside, where you can get acquainted with the traditional lives of the islanders. The first stop on the southern road leading from the capital to the eastern part of the island will allow you to see one of the most famous sights of the island - Pedro St. James Castle in Savannah (open daily, from 9:00 to 17:00, entrance for adults - $ 8, for children - $ 4). It is not a castle but a large and well-fortified mansion. But this is one of the oldest defensive structures in the Caribbean (1780). The castle complex also includes the old Savannah School building and the Visitor Center with a modern multimedia theater.

Continuing along Red Bay Road, you will see the old white lighthouse, which was turned into a restaurant, drive over the ever-noisy surf of the coast at Frank Sound Road or relax on the popular Ram Pound Beach.

Near the island's old capital, the city of Bodden, east of Georgetown, on the main road to the East End, there are Pirates Cave (Pirate Caves). This is a funny place, with its legends and scary stories. The pirates used this place to hide their prey in the numerous damp inner passages of the caves, and the treasures are still in these labyrinths littered with skulls and fragments of some objects.

In the northwest of Grand Cayman, right between the post office and the Hull Clinic, there is another natural attraction of the island - an array of jagged rocks called Hell. This place is like hell! This area attracts thousands of tourists. The southern coast of the district is framed by dozens of resort hotels and first-class dive sites belonging to the Cayman Marine Park, and the northern coast is framed by a long Barker Cay reef.

Nearby is the world's only turtle farm - a true maternity hospital for more than 16 thousand green turtles. This establishment makes great efforts to increase the number of sea turtles in the wild, while there is a sale of meat and shells of turtles. According to the Agreement on International Trade in Endangered Species, the import of products made from the shell of a green sea turtle is prohibited in many countries that have signed this document. So think - do you need to buy a souvenir from the tortoiseshell?... Nevertheless, every year this company produces several thousand small turtles in the sea. And during the breeding season (May - October), farm visitors can witness the egg-laying process (limited access to the farm and the beach is allowed daily, from 8.30 to 17.00).

The center of the eastern part of the island is occupied by the Queen Elizabeth II Botanical Park (open daily from 9:00 to 18:30; admission is $ 7), stretching from the shores of Old Men Bay in the north to Frank Sound Bay in the south. The 65-acre green park is set among the spurs of low hills in an area of enchanting landscape and contains approximately 300 kinds of trees and shrubs growing in the Cayman Islands. The park is famous for its orchids (bloom from May to June), iguanas (you rarely manage to see them), parrots and other birds. A good trail is organized for a walk. Recently, the park has expanded with the Flower Garden and Heritage Garden.

Sea vacation

The western coast of Grand Cayman is famous for its snow-white Seven Mile Beach ("Seven Mile Beach", although in fact, its length is 9 km). Despite a large number of hotels and restaurants, this area can offer vacationers clean white sand, excellent service, and good conditions for diving and all kinds of water sports.

Another good place for a beach holiday and snorkeling is West Bay Cemetery, which lies north of Seven Mile Beach. Nearby is Victoria House Reef, teeming with fish, crustaceans and orange tubular sponges, as well as Trinity Caves, famous for their underwater caves and canyons.

South of the Grand Old House, which lies almost within the capital, there is another popular resort place - the small Smith Cove beach with an abundance of rocky areas and a relatively large difference in depths, and further south begins the Sand Cay reef, famous for its wreck Palace River and diverse marine life.

On the south coast of the island, South Sound Cemetery Beach is especially popular, protected from the sea by the extended Sand Cay reef.

The shores of the east coast abound with sandy beaches surrounded by dozens of resort hotels. The shores of Lower Bay, East Point, Colliers Bay, and Spotter Point can offer both scenic black sand destinations and classic coral beaches, and the road that runs right along the coast allows you to swim in any place you like. The nearby reef creates good conditions for diving, especially attractive in areas north of the lighthouse at Sparrow Hawk Point, as well as near the East End and Ironsawe Point.

The gently sloping northeastern coast sharply turns south in the Ram Point area, where the popular resort area is located. From here, take excursions to the world-famous North Wall reefs and Stingray Sandbar, the most popular attraction of the island, where tourists literally run into three-meter stingrays, sea cats constantly floating in shallow water at the sides of the sightseeing boat in anticipation of a piece of fish or squid that they take directly from the hands of man!

To the south lies the winding Little Sound and Head Sound bays, where you can snorkel among the algae, as well as Water Reef, considered the best place to observe starfish.

Little Cayman Island

Little Cayman Island (Little Cayman) is often referred to as the "Cayman Islands Jewel". Quiet and pastoral islet with an area of only 31 square km and a permanent population of no more than 150 people lies 130 km northeast of Grand Cayman. Almost all of its residents work in tourism, and road signs often recommend giving way to the iguana, which is not surprising as about 2,000 of these animals live on the island. Overgrown with mangroves, wetlands in the center of the island are home to dozens of bird species. Therefore, Little Cayman attracts the attention of tourists seeking solitude in unspoiled nature, as well as scuba divers and outdoor enthusiasts.

The island has a reputation as a great place for beach vacations and dives. Here are wonderful diving sites:

- Jackson Point and North Wall Reef on the northwest coast (the well-known Jackson Marine Park is located on their territory)
- Snape Point Reef in the northeast
- Rosetta Flats and Wiris Bay in the southeast
- the water around the tiny islet of Owen Island
- Preston Bay in the very south of the island
- The famous Bloody Bay Wall reef with depths from zero to 300 meters
- a series of reefs stretching along the entire north-west coast of the bays Spot Bay, Grape Three Bay, and Crawl Bay.

Directly off the coast of the marine park, the possessions of the Birdie-Pound-Nature-Reserve National Bird Sanctuary begin, which is one of the largest colonies of frigate birds in the western hemisphere (the reserve is open for tourists and has a gift shop).

You can also walk along the Salt Rock Niche Trail ecological path and visit the lighthouse on the southwestern tip of the island or Bluff cliffs in the very northeast, from where you can enjoy a panorama of the nearby (10 km) Cayman Brac and the azure blue waters of the Caribbean.

Sea vacation

The best beach areas of Little Cayman lie off the coast of Owen Island's private island (200 meters from Head of Bay), near Point o' Send (Sandy Point) at the easternmost tip of the island, in South Hole Sound Bay, and also in the area of Digereys Point, Rosetta Flat, Grape Three Bay and Crawl Bay. The island's few but modern resort hotels are concentrated on a narrow strip between the Bubby Pound lagoon and the sea.

Cayman Brac

Cayman Brac is the smallest and wildest of the islands of the archipelago, densely overgrown with fruit trees, orchids, and cacti. The island received a name in honor of its most distinctive feature - rocky limestone massif ("brac" in Gaelic denotes a "rocky coastal cliff"), which stretches almost two-thirds of the length of the Cayman Brac, reaching the highest point (30 m) in its easternmost part. With only 1,500 inhabitants, the island is famous for its provincial atmosphere and the amazing friendliness of the islanders and is considered one of the best snorkeling sites!

On the shore, you will find the following attractions:

1. Cayman Brac Museum (open on weekdays from 9:00 to 12:00 and from 13:00 to 16:00, admission is free) in Steak Bay on the north coast of the island
2. Gardens of Christopher Columbus Park North of Aston Ratti Center
3. Peter Cave Caves (in the northeast), Great Cave (at the southeastern tip of the island), Bat Cave, Scall Cave and Rebecca Cave, each of which has a romantic or tragic story
4. Community Park and 180-acre Parrot National Park - Land populated by thousands of birds.
5. A dozen charming houses in a traditional colonial style!

All the other attractions of the island are in the sea!

Most of the Cayman Brac coastline is quite rocky, although there are several sandy shores along the southwest coast. However, you can relax by the sea on the beaches of hotels that are open to all comers or find tiny cozy beaches on the north coast, where there are excellent reefs.

The island has real coral gardens along the southwest coast and an unusual underwater landscape along the east coast, where rocky land cliffs are continued on the seabed in the form of numerous grottoes, caves, and underwater walls!

How to spend time in the Cayman Islands?

Romantic getaway

A romantic tour of the Cayman Islands, to the white sand and coral reefs will be truly amazing! Add to this the colonial charm of the old cities, many great hotels, and wonderful shopping thanks to Duty-Free shops - and your trip becomes just perfect! The best time is winter, when the weather is most favorable for evening walks along the beach.

Have some fun!

Diving. The beauty of coral reefs and wrecks in the depths of the ships. Even if you have never tried scuba diving, this is a great place for the first time. Victoria House, Sand Cay, North Wall, Stingray Sandbar and Water Reef reefs will reveal their secrets to you, and experienced diver guides will help you deal with your gear.

Surfing. The Cayman Islands with their bays and creeks have a huge number of places where you can learn to catch a wave. Surfing here is an integral part of a beach holiday.

Pirate Week. This incredible festival, which lasts from mid-October to the first week of November, will allow you to learn a little more about pirate traditions and have great fun with a big company!

Vacation with children

The Cayman Islands have excellent conditions for families with children. Clean sea, fresh air, plenty of fruits and many exciting places that you and your children will be interested to visit.

Almost every good hotel has children's animation and even babysitting services.

For family holidays with children in the Cayman Islands, Family Recreation and Motorsports Park in Breakers in Grand Cayman are suitable. There are numerous family recreation areas, a small reserve with a botanical garden and a marine farm. And from here you can go to the Mastic Trail hiking trail, passing through relict forests.

Seven Mile Beach and other places with similar conditions are suitable for families with children. Among the places that are definitely worth a visit with the kids is the Pirate Caves. Even an adult will be curious to plunge into the frightening and mysterious world of caves!

An unforgettable adventure will be a flight to the Little Cayman Island in the Birdy Pound National Reserve National Bird Sanctuary or a trip to a turtle farm.

Include a dive to the underwater part of the reef on the Atlantis submarine in the plan of your vacation with children in the Cayman Islands. You will not regret it! The ability to safely show your child the underwater life of a reef will cause a lot of delight in your little ones. The cost of such a walk is USD 70-85 per person.

Beach vacation

Sea holidays in the Cayman Islands consist of three elements. Swimming and beach vacations, surfing and diving. The coral reefs that make up the islands create ideal conditions for any of these activities. The Cayman Islands are divided into beach areas, near each of which hotels have been built that provide all the necessary infrastructure for a better vacation on the sea in the Cayman Islands.

These areas include Seven Mile Beach on the west coast of Grand Cayman, which, despite the abundance of hotels and restaurants, boasts a nine-kilometer strip of white sand. This beach is especially popular with travelers with children due to the shallow-bottom plots. But there are sites with conditions suitable for surfers.

The same can be said of West Bay Cemetery, located north of Seven Mile Beach.

But on the small beach of Smith Cove, the coast is rocky, with significant differences in elevation, and inexperienced swimmers should not climb there.

On the east coast, black sand beaches blend in with coral white. The best places to relax on the beaches in this part of the Cayman Islands are Low Bay, East Point, Colliers Bay and Spotter Point. Another popular Cayman resort area is Ram Point.

A tour to the Cayman Islands with a rest on the sea is impossible without diving. The best diving spots are near Victoria House, Sand Cay, North Wall, Stingray Sandbar and Water Reef.

In Little Cayman, beach areas are concentrated on the shores of Owen Island, a small, private island.

National Cuisine

The national cuisine of the Cayman Islands includes a lot of seafood, cooked in a variety of ways. On the menu of the locals, you will find many exotic fruits. Much of the traditional cuisine of the Cayman Islands was borrowed from Jamaica, under the influence of which they were for a long time.

You can try national dishes of the Cayman Islands in small cafes or in markets. Cayman Islands restaurants prefer European dishes on their menu.

Seafood ceviche. A specialty of the Cayman Islands, which is made from fish or shellfish. Onions and tomatoes are used as additional ingredients.

Steaks from tortoise meat. Like tortoise soup, this unique dish is prepared from the meat of green turtles, which are bred on a local turtle farm.

Tostones. Fried bananas that you can try not only in the Cayman Islands but anywhere in the Caribbean.

Creole pork. Flavored meat cooked with the delicious sauce.

Jerk. Under this name is any jerky in curry sauce.

Side dishes. Fish and meat dishes in the Cayman Islands serve various salads, cakes of cereals or cassava, all kinds of pancakes (the source product can be almost any grain or root vegetables), the fruits of breadfruit, as well as simple side dishes of cassava, rice or peas.

Fish on an open fire. Thus, in the Cayman Islands, they cook red snapper and sea bass, generously pouring lemon juice on the fish.

Cassava pie. The combination of an English baking recipe with a typical island filling is firmly on the menu of many Caribbean islands.

Clam soup. Boiled mollusks of any kind, the islanders willingly eat.

The main drinks of the Cayman Islands are tea and coffee. They are prepared according to many local recipes, with spices and unusual additives. Local beer, rum, and many cocktails are also appreciated. As a snack, they often serve fruits and coconuts.

Shopping

Shopping in the Cayman Islands is a profitable activity as many stores operate here under the duty-free system. In such stores, you can buy many products at low prices.

When shopping in the Cayman Islands I recommend buying:

- Emeralds
- Cuban cigars
- Electronics
- Clothing

Souvenir selling is also popular. First, it is a variety of products from the shells of a green turtle. Turtles are bred on the Cayman Islands themselves. Not far from the capital, there is a turtle farm regularly supplying materials for souvenirs.

Shops in the Cayman Islands are open Monday through Saturday, from 09:00 to 12:00 and from 13:30 to 17:00. On weekends, the work schedule is usually individual, with many duty-free shops open until 24:00 these days. Bargaining on the archipelago is not accepted even in the markets!

There is no sales season in the Cayman Islands!

Printed in Great Britain
by Amazon

19750953R00021